CW01081297

SYLVANIAN FAMILY

Summer Young is a poet from Norwich. She completed a Bachelor's Degree in Creative Writing at The University of Winchester, and now lives in London where she co-runs *Lemon Curd Magazine*. Her work has appeared in *Vortex Literary Journal*, *Asterism Literary Journal*, and *Lemon Curd Magazine*.

Sylvanian Family

Published by Bad Betty Press in 2020
www.badbettypress.com

Cover design by Amy Acre

Printed and bound in the United Kingdom

A CIP record of this book is available from the British Library.

ISBN: 978-1-913268-11-4

Supported using public funding by

ARTS COUNCIL ENGLAND

LOTTERY FUNDED

Sylvanian Family

PRESS

Sylvanian Family

For mum, who sacrificed so much
to carry us through.

Contents

The Clangers

the VCR plays
The Clangers turn to static again

I am in the kitchen, small
amongst the twelve chair table set

the cat places herself on my thighs
she is malting
still I cover my face with her

her purrs mask another man's breathing
my mother's bashing headboard

My Mother as Mount Adrija

some take her their sheep as offerings
watch the blood run from the peak
like candle wax

some lay flat on her soft turf
feel the wind pass over them
the belly of a freezing train

Pyura Chilensis

with the face of a tarsier I climb
from behind the statue
of our hat stand,
step around his invisible shoe
prints—graves,
rabbit snares

the hairdryer hums,
mother is curled on the rug
like a rock

I rest my head on her rump
which is damp,
the swollen belly
of a washed up dolphin

this time I drag her on tarpaulin
through dilatant sand,
to the shore with urchins

I do handstands to please her
but she curls up
pink as a shell,
echoes when the waves hit

No Idea Why They Can Jump So High

'Dads' penises are not like Ken Doll groins'
I wrote in the note-to-self section
of the fridge magnets.

Dad splashed in the rotting boat bath,
lumpy body sloshing
in his microcosmic sea.

His penis graceful as a mole rat,
its nose a star mole,
bloated.

His balls sunken to the bath floor,
excess sack an oil slick above the water.
The finished picture, an atomic bomb.

Plastic fish slipped on soap and fell in.
His sighs made tsunamis to drown them
like God, or a leaf blower to a slug.

I Don't Know Where We Are or Where These Steps Are Going

And there's a real dog like they eat.
I knew once at the top
he was going to fuck me.

The dog is panting, of course
and dribbling—the way
a man salivates
wet strings that stretch
as he watches porn.
I am the porn.
The dog thinks I am a dog.

I wonder if he believes in marriage.
I had had him married already
to my neighbour's dog when we were small
—I don't know if lady dog consented—
he mounted her nonetheless.

They consummated as we ate
ham and crisp sandwiches,
our parents bitching in the kitchen.
We watched long enough to form a memory.

Intermittent Fasting

You remember I held your pinkie
as we watched from the curtain?
Father's hands tight in prayer
around mother's soft neck. You remember
we thought he'd wring her like a chicken?

Your wedding day—Mother sat next to the empty
reservation, her quivering hands
giving you away. White knuckles
clutched the programme with bad print.
Remember as you danced
out of our father's name,
mum collapsed—beautiful workhorse
with his broken world on her back.

My Father as Danny DeVito

I think if he found me now
my father would resemble Danny DeVito
only Danny DeVito's ex-wife
wouldn't own a panic button

Chicken Knickers

Forget the day
that will come
or,
depending when you read this,
the day that has been,
when you walk,
or walked,
into the family bathroom
and you see,
or saw,
your mother
in the bath which is,
or was,
painted like a boat.

Forget that you have seen,
or will see,
her shaving
the nature
off her crotch,
because the man
that calls her
Sex On Legs
likes it.

Forget
that he is not
your father.

Potato Dinner

his mother chewed onions and kicked dogs
unable to read vacancy signs

some rumoured she snapped
her husband's windpipe

Routine

the way dry grass grips and clings
for years to the desert floor
I check the drive each morning
for my father's van

Daddy's Girl, #8

your torch makes the rain
like fireflies
plunging to their death
not that I've seen fireflies

I suspect this is where we might find them
in the forest
or by the box of giraffe toys
or the football shirt you got me
before I knew my times tables

we had something in common
it brushed my knees when I wore it

I turn in the mud
thinking of excuses
for the mother who hates you

leave my parcel,
your parcel, of things
in a shallow grave
moulded from mud
cardboard sagging in the rain

Snapshot

We return to the tropics of the swimming pool.

Dad is in the sauna avoiding pool plasters,
the golfers are in the Jacuzzi with shorts
that hug their groins when they leave the water.
I am eight but this does not disgust me.

They watch my mother through plastic leaves.
She wears a satin bikini, pretends to read.
She never did like the swimming pool.
The golfers picture veins swell on their arms
as they throttle her.

I am on the pool floor and softening—
brother sitting on me—lifeless magic carpet, blue
tiles press against my goggles
lungs shrink with hunger, in the space
of five or six seconds we are all on separate planets
but my mother does not feature
because I would not want to bother her
with drowning

Sylvanian Family

like any good daughter I tie the bed sheets
into a rope for my father
to escape the house he set alight

he returns ten years later
his children charred and crunchy
skin like beef jerky

his ex-wife sits
on the carcass of a sofa
lending her brains to the cockroaches

they explore her skull
like children in a play chamber

My Father as the Flawed Protagonist

when he fell over in 2007
mama laughed
as though he were a curbside stranger

he lay on the gold carpet
like a wounded deer
hoping for a bullet

You Forgot Who You Were When Our Table Lost a Chair

the lamp flickered as though
mourning Benjamin Franklin
or taking the time to praise him

house mouse was not afraid
to run across our patent shoes

on Christmas day I gifted you
with a seat made from matchsticks

we placed it on the table for mouse
next to a doll's house plate

with cheese and milk
and treated him like Father Christmas

Memoirs of a City Fish

you are making potato hash
my mother's recipe

I could make you burn it
if I flew out the window

in my blue towel
I might resemble rain

trick umbrellas
to explode like spots

you would only tie my guts
into a rope

pull me back up
for a taste test

Pica

every night to get myself to sleep
I circle the block
gifting the drains with photos
of women's torsos

my own stomach, so far
from my aorta
gets frostbite
stays heavy

the drains give the photos
the white t-shirt look
beside them, the toilet tissue
I ate for lunch

He's Entitled Because He Watched His Friends Die

one boy swinging perpendicular pushing
the heads of the grass
with dead feet drowning them with red
ants from gaping forearms
the tree branch shakes the blood
drops off the skin as the body bobs
in front of a sunset backdrop,
the other eaten alive
in the mud at a festival
the friends spewed
glitter skipped breakfast to eat
the attention with open mouths,
he's a fundraiser now
for people who die in mud

you saw a sadness in his stained
pillow before he turned you over
and drank you as compensation
your tights hiding in the carpet
outside a weasel pup screams for her dead
mother downstairs his parents correct themselves
with hot drawing pins through the fingertips,
they should have known those boys
would only die and cause trouble

upstairs his hands grow in size as he crushes
your wrists, pubic mound
hitting you like the balls of Newton's
Cradle you worry his parents will hear
your raw skin scraping the carpet
like buttering burnt toast

Fuck You, Eddy

Eddy nailed my cunt to the ground,
the palms of his feet pointing skyward.
Even the lighthouse looked like a cock.

I bled from his dick
and my first period
and the Naland rock underneath my spine.
He had a chip in his left canine.

He took two seconds then passed out
from the pressure in his brain.

Here's what I stole:
wet cigarettes
lighter
some money
a watch

Got a Salmon On

You mount the rocks like an erotic Tarzan.
I am trying to channel my inner bear,
squatting on my own ledge
hands raccooning the fish.

You stand in my peripheral,
dirty briefs and a lot of flesh. A body
that has not endured exercise
but small dinners and holed clothing.

I notice I am breathing.

You are confident like a dog,
just buried your shit in the dirt
like a dog. You catch your salmon
as if it were a plastic bottle.

Notes

'No Idea Why They Can Jump So High' was written in response to Tracey Emin's *No Idea Why They Can Jump So High* (monoprint, 1998)

'I Don't Know Where We Are or Where These Steps Are Going' was written in response to Tracey Emin's *And There's This Real Dog Like They Eat* (monoprint, 1997)

'Chicken Knickers' was written in response to Sarah Lucas' *Chicken Knickers* (photograph, 1997)

'You Forgot Who You Were When Our Table Lost a Chair' was written in response to Tracey Emin's *You Forgot Who You Are* (monoprint, 2012)

'Fuck You, Eddy' was written in response to Tracey Emin's *Fuck You Eddy* (monoprint, 1995)

'Got a Salmon On' was written in response to Sarah Lucas' *Got a salmon on #3* (photograph, 1997)

Acknowledgements

I'd like to thank my family, friends, and all my lecturers and tutors from over the years for their continuing support. Thanks also to Amy and Jake for being so wonderful during this process.

New and recent titles from Bad Betty Press

Rheuma
William Gee

At the Speed of Dark
Gabriel Àkámọ

poems for my FBI agent
Charlotte Geater

The Body You're In
Phoebe Wagner

*And They Are Covered
in Gold Light*
Amy Acre

She Too Is a Sailor
Antonia Jade King

While I Yet Live
Gboyega Odubanjo

The Death of a Clown
Tom Bland

Animal Experiments
Anja Konig

War Dove
Troy Cabida

bloodthirsty for marriage
Susannah Dickey

No Weakeners
Tim Wells

Alter Egos
Edited by Amy Acre
and Jake Wild Hall

Blank
Jake Wild Hall

Raft
Anne Gill

The Dizziness of Freedom
Edited by Amy Acre
and Jake Wild Hall

Forthcoming in 2020

A Terrible Thing
Gita Ralleigh

The Survival Anthology
Edited by Amy Acre
and Jake Wild Hall